AUTOMOBILES

EVERYDAY INVENTIONS

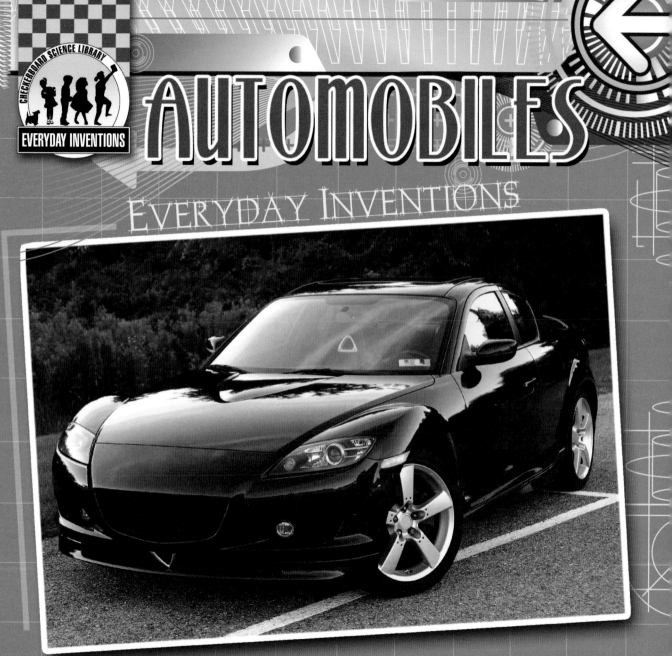

Kristin Petrie

ABDO Publishing Company

visit us at
www.abdopublishing.com

Published by ABDO Publishing Company, 8000 West 78th Street, Edina, Minnesota 55439.
Copyright © 2009 by Abdo Consulting Group, Inc. International copyrights reserved in all
countries. No part of this book may be reproduced in any form without written permission from the
publisher. The Checkerboard Library™ is a trademark and logo of ABDO Publishing Company.

Printed in the United States.

Cover Photo: Getty Images
Interior Photos: AP Images pp. 9, 25, 29; Corbis pp. 5, 8, 11, 23; iStockphoto pp. 1, 13, 14, 15, 21,
    24; Photo Researchers p. 10; PhotoEdit pp. 18, 26

Images on pages 12–13, 16–17, 19 adapted from THE WORLD BOOK ENCYCLOPEDIA.
    © 2007. By permission of the publisher. www.worldbookonline.com

Series Coordinator: Megan M. Gunderson
Editors: Heidi M.D. Elston, Megan M. Gunderson, BreAnn Rumsch
Art Direction & Cover Design: Neil Klinepier

Library of Congress Cataloging-in-Publication Data

Petrie, Kristin, 1970-
  Automobiles / Kristin Petrie.
      p. cm. -- (Everyday inventions)
  Includes bibliographical references and index.
  ISBN 978-1-60453-083-4
  1. Automobiles--Juvenile literature. I. Title.

  TL147.P47 2009
  629.222--dc22

                                          2008001556

CONTENTS

Automobiles

Cars, trucks, and other things that go vroom are called automobiles. Today, automobiles come in various colors, shapes, sizes, and styles. And, automobiles are made by many different companies in countries across the globe. These include Ford Motor Company, Honda Motor Company, BMW, Tata Motors, and Bugatti Automobiles S.A.S.

The word *automobile* comes from two languages. *Auto* comes from the Greek word for "self." *Mobile* is French for "movable." Put them together and you have self-moving.

Where does the word *car* fit in? Car is from the Celtic word *carr*, which means "chariot" or "wagon." Early automobiles were often called horseless wagons or horseless carriages.

In the past, cars were used mostly for getting from one place to another. Today, they provide more options! Large

People no longer rely on just the radio for entertainment in the car. Today, they can watch movies or satellite television!

family cars can be traveling movie theaters. People can live in motor homes. And, race cars prove just how fast automobiles can go. The world of automobiles is growing and changing every day!

Timeline

1769	French engineer Nicolas-Joseph Cugnot built the first automobile.
1876	Nikolaus August Otto built a four-stroke internal-combustion engine.
1885	Carl Benz used an internal-combustion engine in the first practical car.
1908	Henry Ford introduced the affordable Model T, which became the most common automobile in the world.
1939	Air conditioning was introduced.
1966	The National Traffic and Motor Vehicle Safety Act made safety belts a standard feature.
1970	The Clean Air Act led to improvements in how much pollution automobiles create.

Automobile Facts

○ In the United States, 80 percent of households own at least one automobile. And, Americans are more likely to travel by car for vacation than by any other form of transportation.

○ The first official automobile race was run in 1895 from Paris to Bordeaux, France, and back again. The winners drove an average of 15 miles per hour (24 km/hr) along the 732-mile (1,178-km) course!

○ In 1903, Mary Anderson invented windshield wipers. Before this, drivers had to stop and wipe snow, ice, and rain off their windshields by hand. With Anderson's invention, this could all be taken care of from inside the vehicle.

○ Automobile windshields are made of safety glass. Layers of plastic in the glass prevent broken pieces from flying in every direction during an accident.

Ideas in Motion

Who should we thank for the fun automobiles we see and ride in today? Like most great inventions, the automobile is the combination of many grand concepts. Behind these ideas were extraordinary minds. Let's learn their names.

In 1769, French military engineer Nicolas-Joseph Cugnot built the first automobile. Cugnot used a steam engine to power the vehicle.

Nicolas-Joseph Cugnot's first automobile was large and heavy.

This funny-looking, three-wheeled invention could hold four passengers. It traveled at a speedy 2.25 miles per hour (3.62 km/hr).

Nikolaus August Otto created one of the most important inventions in automobile history. In 1876, he built a four-stroke internal-combustion engine. Today, the four-stroke engine is still used in most gasoline-powered cars.

In 1883, Carl Benz (right) founded Benz & Co. to build engines. Within ten years, the company was producing complete four-wheeled automobiles.

In 1885, Gottlieb Daimler and Carl Benz each built a four-stroke internal-combustion engine that used gasoline. Benz then used the internal-combustion engine in the first practical car. The following year, he received a **patent** for this combination of an engine on three wheels. But, it was Henry Ford that helped make cars affordable for the general public.

Ford became famous for mass-producing automobiles. To put them together, he designed a new moving assembly line.

The Ford Motor Company made its own automobile parts and used assembly lines. This allowed Ford to reduce automobile prices and pay workers higher wages.

This assembly line used a conveyor belt to move parts along. As parts came down the line, workers added them to the cars. Ford's invention cut production costs. It also allowed more cars to be made in less time.

In 1908, Ford introduced the famous Model T automobile. Before the Model T, cars were expensive and few people could buy one. Because of the assembly line, the Model T was affordable. It quickly became the most common car in the world. Between 1908 and 1927, Ford Motor Company produced 15 million Model Ts in the United States.

Automobiles became even more popular throughout the 1900s. They also became safer and more environmentally friendly. Air conditioning was introduced in 1939. In 1966, the National Traffic and Motor Vehicle Safety Act made safety belts a standard feature.

The U.S. Congress also passed the Clean Air Act of 1970. This led to the use of unleaded gasoline and devices that make **exhaust** less harmful.

Automobiles have changed a lot since they were invented. They are continuing to change and improve today!

Today, the United States, Japan, and Germany produce the most automobiles. These nations also have the largest numbers of automobiles in the world. In total, there are currently about 450 million cars on the road worldwide.

Bits and Pieces

An automobile contains many parts that work together to make it function. The **chassis** is the frame of a car. It is what the main car parts are connected to. These parts include the body, the engine, the **suspension**, and the **transmission**.

The body of a car is like a shell with different **compartments**. In cars, these include passenger, engine, and trunk compartments. Today, most vehicles are made from a unitized body. This means the chassis and the body are **welded** together as one piece.

AUTOMOBILE ASSEMBLY

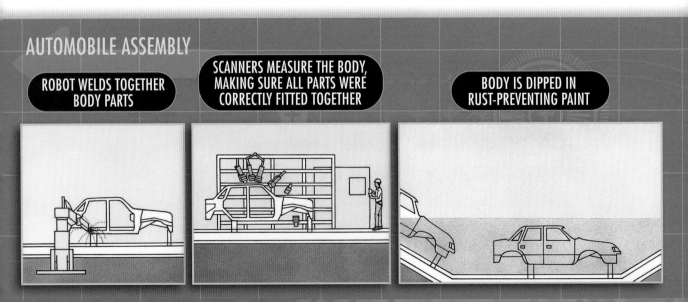

ROBOT WELDS TOGETHER BODY PARTS

SCANNERS MEASURE THE BODY, MAKING SURE ALL PARTS WERE CORRECTLY FITTED TOGETHER

BODY IS DIPPED IN RUST-PREVENTING PAINT

A strong chassis is important for the safety of an automobile's passengers.

PAINT AND AUTOMOBILE ARE GIVEN OPPOSITE CHARGES, ATTRACTING THE PAINT TO THE BODY FOR AN EVEN COAT

ALL OTHER PARTS ARE ATTACHED TO BODY, INCLUDING CHASSIS, ENGINE, WHEELS, AND WINDOWS

WORKERS ASSURE VEHICLE QUALITY THROUGHOUT ASSEMBLY

The engine is an automobile's power producer. It changes air and liquid fuel into motion. Controlled explosions take place inside the engine. Therefore, it is called an internal-combustion engine.

Thanks to the engine, an automobile has the power to move. But an engine can't move an automobile that doesn't

A tire's tread is made up of slits called sipes, as well as deeper grooves. The tread pattern affects how well tires handle different road conditions.

Important controls are all conveniently placed near the driver's seat.

have wheels. The wheels have air-filled tires fitted around them. These **pneumatic** tires make your ride smoother.

To drive a car, you need to use a few instruments. No, we're not talking about drums and guitars! A car's most important instruments include the steering wheel and the gas and brake pedals. These control the car's movement.

Controls for the windshield wipers and headlights are also located within reach of the driver's seat. The dashboard includes dials that indicate speed and how much gas is left. Of course if you want musical instruments, there is always the radio!

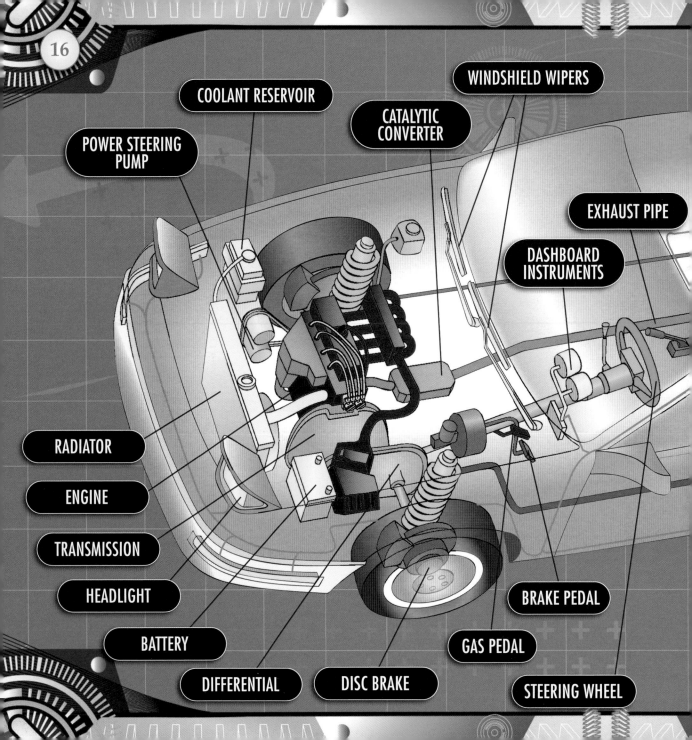

POWER STEERING PUMP

COOLANT RESERVOIR

CATALYTIC CONVERTER

WINDSHIELD WIPERS

EXHAUST PIPE

DASHBOARD INSTRUMENTS

RADIATOR

ENGINE

TRANSMISSION

HEADLIGHT

BATTERY

DIFFERENTIAL

DISC BRAKE

GAS PEDAL

BRAKE PEDAL

STEERING WHEEL

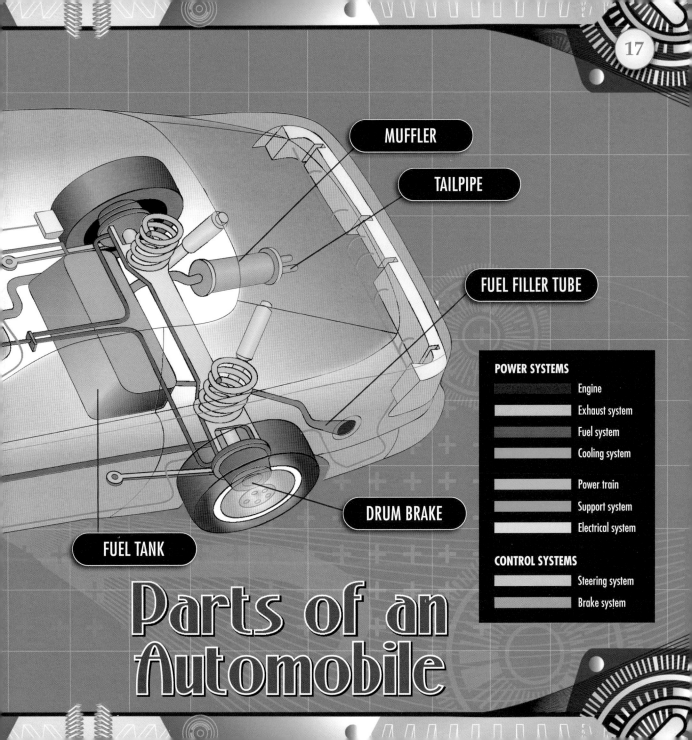

MUFFLER

TAILPIPE

FUEL FILLER TUBE

DRUM BRAKE

FUEL TANK

POWER SYSTEMS

Engine

Exhaust system

Fuel system

Cooling system

Power train

Support system

Electrical system

CONTROL SYSTEMS

Steering system

Brake system

Parts of an Automobile

Start Your Engines

How does an automobile work? When the driver turns the key, electricity flows from the battery to the starting motor. The starting motor spins the **flywheel**, which turns the **crankshaft**.

This makes the **pistons** move, which causes the engine to spark and the car to start. Once the engine is running, the process of converting gasoline to motion begins.

The fuel injection system brings together gasoline from the fuel tank and air. The gas and air meet at the engine's **cylinders** to begin the internal-combustion process. They are combined in just the right proportions so the car is as **efficient** as possible.

Engines are housed in an engine block. This can be located at the front, middle, or back of an automobile.

Each **cylinder** has a **piston**. In most cars, the piston moves up and down the cylinder in a four-stroke cycle. These are the intake, **compression**, power, and **exhaust** strokes.

At each engine cylinder, a fuel pump brings fuel to an injection nozzle. There, the fuel is broken down into a fine mist so that it mixes well with the air. Then, a valve opens into the cylinder. Finally, the mixture goes through the combustion process.

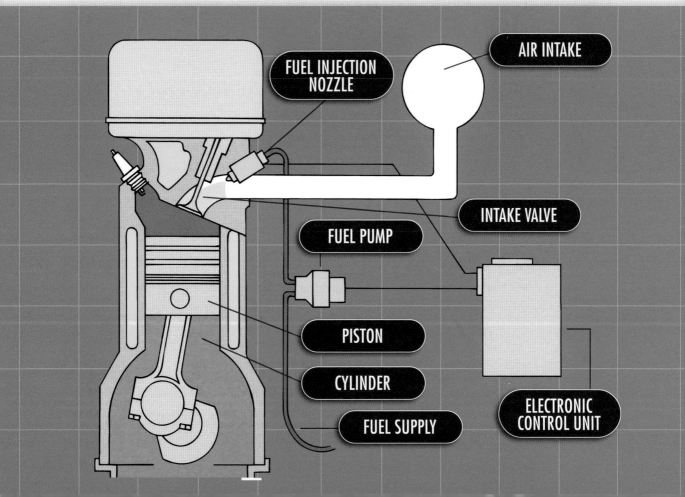

FUEL INJECTION NOZZLE

AIR INTAKE

INTAKE VALVE

FUEL PUMP

PISTON

CYLINDER

ELECTRONIC CONTROL UNIT

FUEL SUPPLY

During the intake stroke, the **piston** moves down the **cylinder**. This pulls in the air and gas mixture. In the second stroke, the piston moves back up the cylinder. This **compresses** the air and the gas.

Next, a **spark plug ignites** the mixture and combustion occurs. This mini explosion pushes the piston down for the power stroke. Last, the piston moves back up the cylinder. This pushes the **exhaust** out of the engine.

In the four-stroke engine cycle, each combustion stroke creates power. This turns the **crankshaft** and the **flywheel**, which send power to the drive train.

The drive train, or power train, moves power from the engine to the wheels. An automobile's drive train handles either two or four of its wheels. This depends on whether the car has front-, rear-, or four-wheel drive.

The power train is made up of the **transmission** and the drive system. The transmission gets power from the engine. It controls the engine's speed.

The drive system takes power from the transmission and sends it through the **differential**. The differential may be attached to the rear **axle**. Or, it may be in the front with the

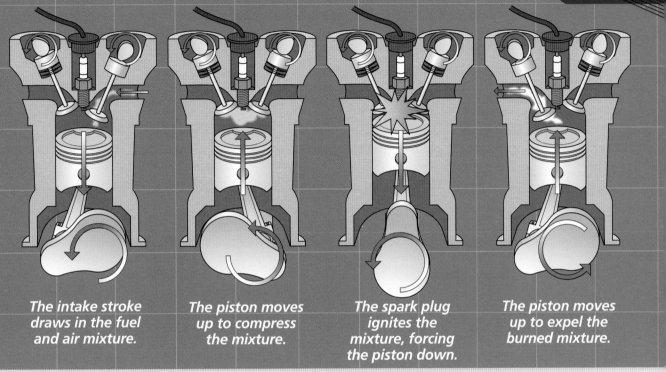

Automobiles generally have between 2 and 12 cylinders. The internal-combustion process takes place in each of these cylinders.

The intake stroke draws in the fuel and air mixture.

The piston moves up to compress the mixture.

The spark plug ignites the mixture, forcing the piston down.

The piston moves up to expel the burned mixture.

engine and the **transmission**. The **differential** allows the wheels to turn at the correct speeds.

Combustion doesn't just create power, it creates heat! So, cars must have a cooling system. This includes **coolant**, a coolant pump, and a radiator. The coolant pump moves coolant around the hot **cylinders** to cool them. Then, the hot coolant flows through the radiator. This process cools it off so the cycle can begin again.

Meanwhile, the lubrication system keeps these systems running smoothly. An oil pump spreads a film over an engine's moving parts. Extra oil is stored in the oil pan, filtered, and reused.

An internal-combustion engine creates **exhaust**. Exhaust needs to be cleaned before leaving the vehicle. It exits the engine through a pipe system called the exhaust manifold.

Exhaust then travels to the car's catalytic converter. This makes it less harmful. Finally, the **muffler** cools the exhaust before it leaves the automobile through the tailpipe.

To move in the right direction, a car requires a good steering system. This is a combination of gears. The steering wheel turns the pinion gear, which turns the rack gear. The rack gear pushes or pulls on tie rods attached to each wheel. This causes the wheels to turn the same direction the driver turned the steering wheel.

Today, most cars have power steering. This means the driver does not have to use his or her own strength to turn the wheels. Instead, the engine's power helps move the gears between the steering wheel and the wheels.

Last but not least are the brakes. Cars often have disc brakes on the front wheels and drum brakes on the rear wheels. When the driver presses the brake pedal, brake fluid sends pressure to the brake pads or shoes. These create **friction** against the car's drums or discs. This pressure stops the wheels from turning.

Automobiles may have disc brakes on all four wheels.

Work and Play

Today, many types of automobiles share the roadways. Automobiles may be grouped by size, style, or usage. For example, passenger cars have four wheels. They usually carry up to six people. Vans and other bigger vehicles are made to carry more than six people.

Most SUVs have four-wheel drive, so the engine powers all four wheels. This helps these vehicles perform well off-road.

Sport-utility vehicles (SUVs) may also carry a large number of passengers. And, SUVs are made to travel on more than pavement. They can easily handle mud, snow, and other rugged surfaces.

Some motor vehicles carry goods, or cargo. If your car stops running, a tow truck may take it to a repair shop. Trucks with refrigerated **compartments** may carry foods such as meat and vegetables to restaurants and stores. These vehicles have stronger engines than regular cars.

Automobiles also can be classified by the type of fuel they use. Electric automobiles run solely on electricity from fuel cells or batteries. Energy from the motor or plugging the car into an electrical outlet can recharge the batteries.

Hybrid cars combine two or more types of power. Many hybrids use electricity and gasoline. These power sources are used together or separately at different times when driving.

Common hybrid cars often have both a gasoline engine and an electric motor.

Designer to Driver

Automobile designers work hard to create exciting new styles that will attract buyers.

Do you love cars? There are many interesting and challenging ways to work in the automobile industry. Designers make some cars look cool and sleek. They make others roomy, with comfortable seats. Above all, designers ensure that automobiles are **streamlined** and safe.

Other people help build cars. On an assembly line, workers may put together various car parts. Or, they may check the quality of work and parts handled by machinery.

After an automobile is built, it must be sold. Drivers deliver automobiles to car lots. There, salespeople tell customers the benefits of each automobile.

Once purchased, service and repair people keep cars running smoothly. Together, these workers help the automobile industry grow and succeed.

Do you wish you could fly down the road in a fast car? Drag racers go 300 miles per hour (480 km/hr) or more on a straight track. They use parachutes to slow down!

Stock cars look like normal automobiles. But, they are much heavier and have more powerful engines. They race in laps on oval tracks. Formula One racing cars have their engines in the back. These specially designed automobiles race on road courses.

Positive Outlook

How do cars affect your life? Obviously, they help you get places faster. You can go farther and see more than you would if you had to walk everywhere. The automobile industry also creates jobs for millions of people worldwide.

Unfortunately, the convenience of automobiles has its price. Automobiles cause noise pollution. Car engines create **exhaust**, which causes air pollution. And, gasoline is expensive and in limited supply.

However, car manufacturers are designing cars that are better for our society. Many new automobiles are quieter. They also use less fuel and keep dangerous fumes out of the air.

You can do something, too! Carpool with friends, ride your bike, and walk when you can. These simple choices will help decrease the negative effects and increase the positive effects of automobiles on our society.

The futuristic, ultracompact Toyota i-unit runs on batteries. It is also made of environmentally friendly materials. The seat reclines for high-speed driving. And, drivers can change the color of the vehicle. Maybe one day, cars such as these will be common on your street!

GLOSSARY

axle - a shaft or a bar on which a pair of wheels revolves.

chassis (CHA-see) - a supporting frame, such as that of a car or an aircraft.

compartment - a section within an enclosed space.

compress - to squeeze together and reduce in size, especially to make fit in a smaller space. Compression is the process of compressing something.

coolant - a mixture of water and antifreeze.

crankshaft - a shaft driven by a crank. In an automobile engine, the crankshaft changes the up-and-down motion of the pistons into the rotary motion needed to drive the wheels.

cylinder - a solid figure of two parallel circles bound by a curved surface. A soda can is an example of a cylinder.

differential - a system of gears that allows one wheel of an automobile to revolve at a different speed than another wheel during a turn.

efficient - wasting little time or energy.

exhaust - used gas or vapor that escapes from an engine.

flywheel - a heavy wheel that moderates the speed of an automobile engine.

friction - the force that resists motion between bodies in contact.

hybrid - combining two or more functions or ways of operation.

ignite - to set on fire.

muffler - a device that makes an exhaust system less noisy.

patent - the exclusive right granted to a person to make or sell an invention for a certain period of time.

piston - a cylinder fit inside a hollow cylinder in which it moves back and forth. It is moved by or against fluid pressure in an engine.

pneumatic (nu-MA-tihk) - filled with compressed air.

spark plug - a part of an internal-combustion engine that fits into a cylinder. It causes an electrical spark, which ignites the fuel and air mixture.

streamlined - designed to reduce drag or resistance to motion when moving through air or water.

suspension - a system of devices that suspends, or supports, the upper part of an automobile on the axles.

transmission - a series of devices that move power from the engine to the wheels of an automobile.

weld - to join metal parts using heat.

WEB SITES

To learn more about automobiles, visit ABDO Publishing Company on the World Wide Web at **www.abdopublishing.com**. Web sites about automobiles are featured on our Book Links page. These links are routinely monitored and updated to provide the most current information available.

INDEX

A
air conditioning 11
assembly line 10, 27
axle 20

B
battery 18, 25
Benz, Carl 9
BMW 4
brakes 23
Bugatti Automobiles S.A.S 4

C
careers 26, 27, 28
catalytic converter 22
chassis 12
Clean Air Act 11
coolant 21
coolant pump 21
crankshaft 18, 20
Cugnot, Nicolas-Joseph 8
cylinders 18, 19, 20, 21

D
Daimler, Gottlieb 9
differential 20, 21

E
engine 8, 9, 12, 14, 18, 20, 21, 22, 25, 27, 28
exhaust 11, 19, 20, 22, 28

F
flywheel 18, 20
Ford, Henry 9, 10
Ford Motor Company 4, 10
four-stroke cycle 9, 19, 20, 21
fuel 9, 11, 14, 15, 18, 20, 25, 28

G
gears 22

H
headlights 15
Honda Motor Company 4

M
Model T 10
muffler 22

N
National Traffic and Motor Vehicle Safety Act 11

O
oil 22
oil pump 22
Otto, Nikolaus August 9

P
pedals 15, 23
pistons 18, 19, 20

R
radiator 21

S
safety belts 11
spark plugs 20
starting motor 18
steering wheel 15, 22
suspension 12

T
tailpipe 22
Tata Motors 4
tie rods 22
tires 15
transmission 12, 20, 21

W
wheels 8, 9, 15, 20, 21, 22, 23, 24
windshield wipers 15